Zippety Zoo

By Katharine Kenah

School Specialty.
Publishing

Library of Congress Cataloging-in-Publication Data is on file with the publisher.

Send all inquiries to:
School Specialty Publishing
8720 Orion Place
Columbus, OH 43240-2111

ISBN 0-7696-4264-0

1 2 3 4 5 6 7 8 9 10 PHXBK 10 09 08 07 06 05

D0043722

Hi, I'm Marsupial Sue.
Join me in learning about what goes on at a zoo!
Animals live in many different places around the world.
Some animals live in the wild.
Some animals live in people's homes.
Some animals live in a zoo.
Grab your camera and hop along with me.
We are about to explore the Zippety Zoo.

Table of Contents

Reptile House

You see something move under the leaves.
You hear jaws snap.
It is daytime in the **reptile** house at the zoo.
Lizards, snakes, turtles, tortoises, crocodiles,
and alligators all live in the reptile house.
Reptiles are cold-blooded.
Their body temperatures change
to match their surroundings.
If their homes are cold, their bodies are cold.
If their homes are warm, their bodies are warm.
Reptiles will die if they get too cold or too hot.
So, zoo reptiles move back and forth
between the shade and sunny spots
until their body temperatures are just right.

Marsupial Sue Shares

Some snakes swallow small animals whole.

Giant Cats

Resting on rocks or hiding in the grass,
the giant cats watch every move you make.
This zoo **exhibit** is home to some
of the world's fiercest predators.
Lions, tigers, jaguars, panthers,
cougars, leopards, and cheetahs roam this space.
These large cats are like hunting machines.
They are quick and very strong.
Giant cats are **carnivores**.
They hunt and eat other animals.
Their good eyesight allows them
to hunt in the dark.
To keep the other zoo animals safe,
the giant cats have their own space at the zoo.

Marsupial Sue Shares

A zoo lion can live to be 25 years old. A lion in the wild usually
lives for only 12 years.

Tropical Rain Forest

The air is steamy and warm.
Trees and plants are thick around you.
Birds squawk.
Insects buzz.
You are in the zoo's tropical rain forest.
Tropical rain forests are home to some of the
world's most important **natural resources**.
Tropical rain forests form a green band
around the center of the earth.
But this zoo exhibit brings the forest to you.
Parrots and toucans flap their wings.
Orchids grow on the trunks of trees.
Brightly colored butterflies and tiny frogs
look like gems against the dark green plants.

Marsupial Sue Shares

Tropical rain forests cover a very small amount of the earth's
surface, but they are home to more than half of the world's
plant and animal species.

Aquarium

Thousands of gallons of water surround you.
Inches away, a school of yellow and silver
fish swims by.
Inside the zoo's aquarium,
you can experience what life is like under water.
An aquarium houses thousands
of **aquatic** plants and animals.
Starfish and sea anemones look like flowers
in an undersea garden.
Sharks glide past the large glass windows.
Dolphins and porpoises leap out of their pools.
A killer whale rises out of the water to catch a fish.
Sea lions sleep in the sun on a ledge.
Seals do belly flops into the water.

Marsupial Sue Shares

Most starfish have only five arms, but some have as many
as forty!

African Plains

The sun beats down.
A dry wind blows across the grass.
You might feel hot,
but the animals of the African plains
are at home in this part of the zoo.
They are used to a hot and dry **climate**.
This zoo exhibit is designed
to look and feel just like the African plains.
A hippopotamus cools off in the water.
Three giraffes stand under a tree,
using their tongues to grab tree leaves.
A herd of zebras stands close together,
watching a rhinoceros nearby.
The sights of Africa are all around you!

Marsupial Sue Shares

Giraffes are the tallest animals in the world. Male giraffes can grow to be 18 feet tall. This is almost as tall as a two-story house.

Bear Den

You have just entered the zoo's bear den.

A brown bear scratches its back on a tree stump.

A sun bear sleeps on a rock in the sunshine.

A giant panda sits alone, eating bamboo shoots.

A grizzly bear holds a frozen fish

between its huge paws.

Bears are large mammals with big heads,

bulky bodies, and powerful legs.

Thick coats of fur cover their bodies.

Bears are **omnivores**.

They eat both plants and animals.

During cold months, many bears **hibernate**

in caves or dens.

Marsupial Sue Shares

Some bear cubs weigh only half a pound when they are born, as much as two sticks of butter. They have no fur, and their eyes are closed.

15

Animals Down Under

The animals in this exhibit are
from the "Land Down Under."
This land is Australia.
Australia is a large island **continent** in the middle
of the Indian and Pacific oceans.
You will see unusual animals, such as the platypus,
dingo, emu, black swan, and Tasmanian devil,
living there.
You will also see some of Australia's
famous **marsupials**.
Kangaroos, koalas, wombats, and wallabies
all live in Australia.
These animals are tiny and helpless
when they are born.
They grow in pouches on their mothers' stomachs
until they are strong.

Marsupial Sue Shares
Koalas can eat 20 pounds of eucalyptus leaves in one day.

Aviary

Parrots shriek.
Owls hoot.
A peacock spreads its tail,
looking like a fan of green and gold.
You are in the zoo's aviary.
An aviary houses all different kinds of birds.
They fly through the air.
They rest in trees.
They build nests.
High above the trees and plants,
a wire net keeps the birds from flying away.
Some of the birds in the aviary are **endangered**.
There are very few of them left in the world.
An aviary keeps them safe
so that they do not disappear from nature.

Marsupial Sue Shares

The male peacock's beautiful tail feathers are about five times
as long as its body.

Primate House

A huge gorilla sits by the glass window.
His eyes follow every movement
the crowd makes.
You are in the zoo's **primate** house.
Monkeys, apes, gorillas, chimpanzees,
gibbons, orangutans, and baboons live here.
Primates are intelligent animals with large brains.
They have hands that can grasp
and pick things up.
Most primates also have long arms and tails.
This helps them climb and move
from tree to tree.
Most primates are **arboreal**.
They live in trees.

Marsupial Sue Shares

Gorillas have been taught to communicate with trainers using
American Sign Language.

Elephant House

In the elephant house,
giant animals are on the move!
Elephants are among the biggest mammals on earth.
An elephant's trunk is part nose and part lip.
Elephants breathe, smell, and drink with their trunks.
They also use their trunks like hands to pick things up.
There are two different kinds of elephants.
African elephants have big, flat ears
that cover their shoulders.
Indian elephants are slightly smaller.
They have smaller ears and two humps
on the tops of their heads.
Indian elephants are also known
as "Asian Elephants."

Marsupial Sue Shares

An adult elephant's skin measures 1 ½ inches thick–as thick as tree bark. But an elephant can still feel the bites from bugs.

Butterfly Garden

The air is warm.
Dots of color dart quickly around you.
You are inside the zoo's butterfly garden.
Thousands of butterflies live
in this exhibit.
Butterflies come in all different
sizes and colors.
Small, flat scales cover a butterfly's wings.
These scales give butterflies
their beautiful colors and patterns.

Marsupial Sue Shares

There are almost 20,000 different kinds of butterflies in the world. The largest butterfly, the Queen Alexandra's birdwing, lives in Papua New Guinea. It has a wingspan of 11 inches—almost as big as a ruler!

Zoo Nursery

You are in the zoo's nursery.
A zoo nursery is home
to all kinds of baby animals.
This is where the babies of the zoo are taken care of.
Veterinarians keep the babies healthy
and care for them when they are sick.
They study the babies
to make sure they develop properly.
Some animals in the zoo nursery
are the babies of animals living in the zoo.
Others are the babies of animals
living in the wild.
Some endangered animals are in danger
of vanishing from the world.
Zoos care for their babies to make sure
this doesn't happen.

Marsupial Sue Shares

The Bronx Zoo in New York had the first zoo nursery. It was
opened in 1944 to care for three tiger cubs.

Zookeeper

Who is holding that animal?
It is a zookeeper.
A zookeeper is trained to take care of
animals at a zoo.
Zookeepers feed and water
the animals under their care.
They wash and **groom** them.
They make sure that the animals get lots
of fresh air and exercise.
Zookeepers also train the animals.
They watch the animals closely
to make sure that they are healthy and safe.
Zookeepers take care of the animals' homes, too.
They also talk to zoo visitors about the animals
and answer their questions.

Marsupial Sue Shares

Zookeepers are often trained as biologists first. In the United
States, there are fewer than 5,000 zookeepers.

Vocabulary

aquatic–an animal or plant that lives in water. *A dolphin is an aquatic animal.*

arboreal–living in a tree. *A monkey is an arboreal animal.*

carnivore–an animal that eats other animals. *A panther is a carnivore.*

climate–the weather conditions of a place. *The climate of the African plains is warm and dry.*

continent–one of the earth's seven main bodies of land. *We live on the continent of North America.*

endangered–a plant or animal in danger of no longer existing. *The black bear is an endangered animal.*

exhibit–something that is created as a public display for people to see. *My class went to see the art exhibit at the museum.*

groom–to clean and brush. *The zookeeper grooms the baby elephant.*

hibernate–to sleep through the winter to save energy. *Bears hibernate during cold weather.*

marsupial–a mammal of the order Marsupialia found mainly in Australia. *A kangaroo is a marsupial.*

natural resources–materials found in nature that are used by people in many ways. *Forests are important natural resources.*

omnivore–an animal that eats both plants and animals. *Bears are omnivores.*

primate–a mammal of the order Primates, including monkeys, apes, and human beings. *Ryan studied primates in his biology class.*

reptile–an animal with scaly skin and an internal skeleton arranged around a backbone. It breathes air through its lungs. *I made a clay model of my favorite reptile in art class.*

veterinarian–a doctor who treats animals. *We took our sick dog to the veterinarian.*

Think About It!

1. What kinds of animals live in the zoo's reptile house?

2. What kinds of animals live in the giant cat exhibit?

3. What does *arboreal* mean?

4. Why are tails and long arms useful to primates?

5. How are African and Asian elephants different?

The Story and You!

1. How would your life be different if you were cold-blooded like a reptile? Or if you were arboreal like a monkey?

2. Which exhibit at the Zippety Zoo is your favorite? Why?

3. If you could design your own zoo exhibit, which animals would you include in it?

4. If you could be a zookeeper, which animal would you like to take care of? Why?

5. Think about a school of fish that you might see at an aquarium. What are some similarities between this school and your own school?